Pavans

IAN KRIEGER

OMMATION PRESS

For Loren, Darryl, Anick, Tom & Carol

OMMATION PRESS
5548 N. Sawyer
Chicago, Illinois 60625

Illustration: Sarah Micklem
Photo: Darryl Golden

ISBN 0-941240-00-2

Library of Congress Cataloging in Publication Data

Krieger, Ian, 1948–
    Pavans.

    (Dialogues on dance ; #3)
    1. Dancing--Poetry. I. Title. II. Series.
PS3561.R553P3 1985   811'.54   84-22660

© 1985 by Ian Krieger/Ommation Press

Sometimes I think of all of us as dances.

CYCLE ONE

Pavan 1
 (for Anick)

Owl's half-
mooned light
on

shoulder
blades.

Fever-scraped
cheeks,

the tenderness
of indoor heating.

Bow from
proud torso.

Courtesy
to cold faun.

Grey squirrel
climbing

bare oak.

The once dark
ages.

Pavan 2
  (for Maureen)

Comprehending the works
of New York
while a chameleon runs

through motion's loft.

(Imbalanced Balinese color.)

An essay of architectural space.
A distribution of style
via congregation.

To dance Duchamp-

"when the music begins
proceed in any which way

as facilitates
a tangle."

Pavan 3
   (for Carol)

Stiff new leather
shoes on the buffed
floors of Milan.

Scratchy styles
from the '30's.

Motion pronounced
by the seasonal parity
of words.

Sky rolling different weights
in January and June.

Body a feeling notched by memory.

How to bring your partner
into focus.

Your new white shoes.

How you color your cheeks
with flowers

for the first time.

Pavan 4
   (for Lynn)

Pails catch
white.
Golden Koi
rub against
the bitter taste
of tin.

Frozen crickets,
frozen night,
frozen moon.

Snow to set air.
Pails to set snow.

Tin set,
eyes set,
mouths set.

Bitter catch.

Cold Koi
rub against
cold crickets.

Old taste,
snow taste,
rubs against
the taste within.

Pavan 5
  (for R.)

See me in summer
clothes.
Move—

over Death.

It's not a shadow dance.

Your partner's
up for grabs.

I'm butting in.

Pavan 6
  (for C.)

Phaedra for a day
then back again
to routine.

Appalachian window light
shades into rain.

Begin with torso
on floor.

See space
not body
knotting air.

Crave balance
when all else
spins.

How myth grows
from ceramic mud.

Exiled from complication
dew empties your sleeves
and is gone.

Pavan 7
  (for Tom S.)

Scarecrow in
a field of
cornflowers.

Wrapping by contour.

Worlds of cast iron,
rust,
and scrap.

The death of statues.

Black oxidation
because strung wires
merely connect.

The history of gardens
is the point.

Taxonomy needs
a moving language.

All things dance,
if only in

juxtaposition.

Pavan 8
  (for Gene and Jean)

Rose's microclimate
in earth light
calibrates newness
to eye.

When Babel fell
language wasn't deepest loss.

Art orders a gibberish
that's far from new,

stills the primal fear

that chaos comes colorless
like a hip injury.

Pavan 9
 (for Darryl)

Sight's trade route
behind

selected objects.

Location bartered
from sensation.

Sexual mystery,
shadows on silver,

platinum prints.

Shifting microcosms
fashion scale.

Possibility
a stimulant,

a dance
ranging from sage

to the musk of pinion.

Rain on adobe.
A pruning light.

The pirouette of
home-baked bread.

Pavan 10
   (for John)

Ahab
on splintered deck
above spellbound
grey sea

had nothing
on your silence.

Sun streaks
migrating

breaking surface wave
for air

keeps you
in motion.

Posture set
by blood's salt.

When the joints of
whalebone creak

always the quiet one

to hear
glacier's death
in their song.

Pavan 11
  (for Lynn)

As circles
to the feet

wait partners,

baseboards
and windows

sometimes beside.

Moving stars over
tawdry storm.

How still your ankles
and bent knees

in the rain.

Pavan 12
  (for N.)

Spin,

a spiral path
of large pitch

and small radius.

Oh, evening,

comes like a shell's edge
to loneliness.

Turning,
yearning like Shaker's
celibacy.

Oh, morning,

comes a disc white sun
over clover grey,

comes aching
like smartweed
or water pepper,

to see you
at the apex

of your motion.

Pavan 13
  (for C.)

Coyly scouring tempo
encompasses

and we pass
invisible,

as slow as emptiness.

Desire proclaims no guarantee
against rondelet.

Emotional
by partnering

we become the sun,
rediscovered,

unfamiliar and literal
in

motion.

Pavan 14
  (for T.)

Thermal dancing
in an oblong room.

A tragic love holding tight
the God-cold evenings.

Your almond eyes
hushing the harsh

imbalanced core heights
of my body.

Pavan 15
  (for Tom A.)

Motets of change
see sound
as ripples
in the Chinese.

Like the sparse hands
of John Cage

they can tune
the waves of a piano

to a nail.

Pavan 16
  (for Nancy)

Salome in pants
passes for the buzzing

in John the Baptist's mind.

He sought to still the dervish
by water,

while the dervish in her
spun sex

that she had to encircle with flesh
or lose.

(We all are chosen or chose
to be born again.)

Only she cut the cord
of what she once loved

by dancing.

Pavan 17
   (for Anick)

Heraclitus isn't text,
but motion.

Oxygen and cut crystal,
sweet bubbles in champagne,

slope of temperature,
space in rain,
foil in sunlight,

all whisper.

Pavan 18
   (for Sally)

Circles of breeze,
ringlets of air.

Copper bracelets
on a fine-haired
tanned arm.

A lacquer of L.A.

You,
without Noh mask,

court dancing.

Pavan 19
  (for N.)

Cigarette smoke
on bare air.

The oldest Muse
is memory.

When by steps
brightness rises

winter ends.

Your cheeks in spring
hot with the presence

of sex in man.

Pavan 20
   (for Salvador)

She teaches legs
to tie knots,

to climb her world
from toes up.

Passing ankles,
passing thighs,

passing fingers
with their silver
and jade rings.

Passing her linen blouse
and her sweat bands of pearls.

Higher than her kinky hair.

Her eyes stranded.

She makes your sneakers
and boots

rise.

She calls out steps
that empty

your shoes.

Pavan 21
   (for Carol)

Airport,
its grey astringent ground.

Terminal buildings as islands.

Sun is reggae
streaked across sky.

How pressure undersounds a wing.

How we rise above scale
by jumping moving objects.

Pavan 22
   (for Sam)

Jealousy is clumsy,
always spilling.

Edges to nerves
and you spin.

So there are circles
fumbling to be round.

Dance is the most personal art,
all bodies are unique in air.

Travels through certainty
with no partner.

How life is rhythm
out on shakedown.

Pavan 23
   (for Loren & Laury)

Mind is percussive.

Turn its eye
and you change tuning.

Wrapped in sound
your song is Chagall's
color-borne bride

rising fresh with child

in the wild mountain air
of banjo.

Pavan 24
   (for Llon & Marsha)

She braids the uncombed.
His life badger-like.

They sleep,
footsore travelers,
under goose down
and woodstove smoke.

Their dance a ridgespine
over the trebleness of

rounded mountains.

Their power
clinging to earth
like Rome,

an epithet,

twilight on a rainy day.

Pavan 25
  (for Corey)

Hills instead of light
in winter.

Hot herb tea
across the bare room,

captures arch-grey heights
by aroma.

Perspective being
the taxonomy of time.

The trick to leaping
is not in staying up,

but coming down
as slowly as a bat

from sleep.

CYCLE TWO

Pavan 26
  (for C.)

Insteps withhold mystery.

Close body contact;
suddenly the game of tracking

leads to tenderness.

How to dress for dance
by turning.

Balance for motion,
or grace to hide.

Discipline and want
being but bass line and melody

to love.

How hard won steps vanish,

or lead
to new realities.

Pavan 27
 (for Kate)

Lucid
taut of heel

where flamenco
edges.

Death
is a faked emotion.

To never be silenced
or forced to move

by another's
pretended motion

or stillness.

To have force enough
to dislodge grief.

Passion enough
to undo

the ache of blood.

Pavan 28
  (for Tom)

I'm glad I know Sappho
if only by reputation.

Eros is luscious here,
taunts me.

This light's hot sound
strips color off orchids and palms.

Events move fast,
more cinema than simile,

a camera pace,
a demand for fashion
that makes style appear.

Image craves
a modern meter.

Tanned bodies dance
in sun's beat.

Here rumor replaces literature.

Language, arises from motif,

intimate and opaque
from sensual light.

Sappho would have loved L.A.,
an island city,

a sex that shines
from matter,

a sex that softens
night.

Pavan 29
  (for Christine)

You were cinnamon and day moon,
a cadent desert dancer.

I knew,
as shell white clouds

unsheathed shadows
over foothills,

that joining your dance
was joy.

But awkward, word struck,
earth-bound,

burdened by in-faced gait,
I wilted.

My rhythm wavered,
tapped,

stuck like dust on wood.

Now that distance
from unconsciousness to
native state,

from dry white moon
to culled green eyes,

fades like a slowly gathered herb,

and my desire for you
unwraps

like a wavering star
in a sextant.

Pavan 30
  (for J.)

Branch bare maple
and oak

tell of coming.

Fluent voice,
inflection of snow in wind,

quiet of
the leatherbound book
on the oiled wood shelf.

The last pear's eaten.

Here the empty cast of days.
Music an unbleached grey,

light stilled,
a lamentation.

This scar of a pause
a sprung trap.

Oh my love,

strings of night
tie back

the stumble of my desire,

and your absence
is winter.

Pavan 31
  (for L.)

Hear music through
your body's downed beat.

Your failures
might have frozen time,

but it wasn't time
that wouldn't let you leap.

It's always a shifting world.

Being can't freeze it
or we'd escape by seeing.

Essence is grace.

When you dance
you reclaim the world.

Death's not an exterior,
only a will that's atrophied
its music.

You've got music left.

In your eyes
it breathes,

it marks,
it dips.

Sway your loss;
sense your hips

and the rest of the way home
is easy.

Pavan 32
  (for Ilya)

Newborn in
new time,

how slight
your body

that fevers
at the debut
of a tooth,

or clings,
or crawls,
to mine

along the magnetic lines
of affinity.

I watch your first steps
across the floor

and feel the joy
of balance,

as it and language
draw to you
like a breath

before leaping.

Sometimes when I hold you

I feel the world is air,

our bodies
air instead of water.

When you sleep
I exhale.

When you wake
and look at me,

I breathe
the very air

of dance.

Pavan 33
  (for C.)

Because she lives up a hill
climbing is metaphor.

To shift footing
like a wild goat

kept between high fields
and mountain's sky.

Illumination dwells
between crevice
and foreground.

How in direct sun,
or in oak-scented shade,
her figure releases.

(A dream of a stone hut;
hot tea and clove honey
keeping out the storm.)

Because she lives up a hill
metaphor is climbing.

Oblivion is rhythmic.
Space does not rust.

(Nor love.)

Only the body turns from beige to black
and fades away.

Pavan 34
  (for G.)

Muscle beach is lonely
in trauma.

Skeletons of roller coasters
sing the wind.

Light cuts into abandoned buildings.
Echoes map their forms.

Passion excavates
heart's cavity.

Rain clones on dead eucalyptus.

Treachery prefigures loss.

Failures,
ash scattered over sea.

Desire's fury pressed into
descent.

What could have been done
sinks like a book of matches

into a pocket.

So many signs
and stray signals.

Eros turns her best profile
towards sun

for a tan
and a light for her dangling cigarette.

Pavan 35
   (for J.)

Be-
grudge me
nothing
(on time
or late)
eternities
are wavering
(a force of
your breath be-
hind my ear)
out where
the waves
(your knees on
sand-
your hands
and the salt
of this keeping)
are made, and
there is
a moon sink-
ing.
(I taste you
in the kitchen
where colors
stack, scent,
fade.)
The sea
endless but
not for the shore,
and you stroll-
ing with me,
holding no-
thing that I
(who used to fumble)
can't catch

with a word, or gather like
(mussel & clam,
rain & drift-
wood)
sweet balance.
Sometimes bitter
night in
contrasting emotions,
what you and I
go towards
again
(sea fish, shellfish,
Creole spice)
and again.

Pavan 36
  (for Tom A.)

A series of lovers
welcomes you

to Rimbaud city.

Just who was this fellow
Appollin-Baudel-aire,
and why is it his style

we speak?

Oh Sylvia-Anne-Plath-Sexton,
Edgar-Hart-Poe-Crane-Dylan.

Oh T.S. D.H. H.D. Pound-Williams-Yeats,
Robert-Bogan-Levertov-Patchen-Jarrel-
Stevens,

what is language?

Pavan 37
   (for V.)

Sappho in a grove
of olive trees

knew language as blossom,
bud

and fruit.

Style is Mediterranean.

In Brazilian night
the Amazon
is not just a river,

but taste.

While others ridge
you cross between.

While others partner
to conventional sound

you hear wild moon
shaking down high branches,

see Diana
as Diana wishes to be seen,

find Diana
where Diana wishes

to be found.

Pavan 38
   (for Frederique)

City light,
smudged pastel sky,
and I,

lover for an afternoon,

lean past shadow
into a room.

Taste, sound, sight,
the weight of your body.

Wind in day;
how an hour passes.

At times this universe
seems changeless,

lasting as it will last,

with passion, mountain,
kiss, fruit, bush,

alive, yet out of sight.

It's an arrangement
for outflow.

From the ledge I occupy,
from the curve of my back,

an impetus.

But impetus slips between cracks,
behind stairs.

There is this physical trap
that emotion obscures.

It's not that I deny your grace,
or that daylight burns,

but that I see you clearest
across a certain distance.

It's why night feels
right in black,

why shadow and shade
are so exact.

It's the nature of exchange.

Oh, the cold wind pours through the trees
on to our separation,

on to my skin,
which now without you,

suddenly seems to belong
more to this universe

than it does to my body.

Pavan 39
  (for Fred)

Where would we be without floors?

Irregular rooms, curved ceilings,
French doors,

take a chance on light.

Sky detaches,
pools, dries

to the counterpoint
of material and metaphor.

Texture rises from blueprints,
mindprints,

renderings.

Style starts with rhythm.
Souls need boutiques.

Buildings gossip as well as speak.
Form craves a hangout.

Bare wood, terrazzo, granite,
exposure to light,

function leads to excitement.

Freedom from mundane climates,
repetitive rooms,

renatured space,

breeds all-night
dance parties.

Pavan 40
   (for Leonard)

You are breathing media,
industry and automobiles,

pumping Vitamin E.

Plastic was,
and style will be

wearing a gas mask,

caught in a conceptual
traffic jam

between a Los Angeles radio dream
and a sushi bar aesthetique

stolen from
a post-modern Japan.

Pavan 41
 (for Anick)

Moss does not grow
but appears at curious

times.

The idea of moss
is the reality

of shade and water.

Shade is written
by the trees.

Water contrasts
blue to grey

the way that silence
tastes of silence

in a forest.

The poem does not grow
but appears

where moss might grow
if there wasn't

a poem.

Pavan 42
  (for G.)

It suddenly becomes
culture or fiction,

but always fashion.

Excess flashed or trimmed,
padded Crawford shoulders

or the ultramodern.

Pre-Raphaelite embellishment
versus function.

Bric-a-brac versus

(oh the need for interior decoration)

the Bauhaus.

If only minimalism
was an easy act to follow,

or speech tuned enough to a poem
to allow luxury to shape visibility

from signature.

But the trick always seems to flourish
amidst the concealed.

The task being to make style itself
compel the vague,

the vogue,

into the real.

Pavan 43
  (for A.)

Seemingly silent,
perfect,

womanly still.

Do mountains dance?

You,
who others judged to be

lost in the reverie
of ballet

were looking to
tango.

You seemed such a classical rhythm;
how was I to know

you craved the saxophone,
ached for steamy plains.

Rather than the stillness
of pavan

you wanted wild music
to rattle your body

and shake dance
into your brains.

Pavan 44
 (for W.)

She Vogue,

endless photographic runs,
Avedon, Hurrell, Bourdin, Penn,

comes without significance
of sequence.

Art witnesses,
but sex reveals.

Desire animates
while the poet

hisses messages between
the impossible and real.

L.A. is where future thrives,

signs of decadence
shaping passion into lives.

Reality, dream, and time
move along the same meridian.

Metaphor substitutes,
a Duchampian pun.

Fashion tunes to wavering.

Stolen image, stylish hair,
trendiness in severe lines,

aesthetics all decked out
for fame before its time.

She runs in breathless spurts
like a camera,

while I accelerate
to grasp the secret messages

of her plagiarism.

Pavan 45
   (for Claudette)

Palms sultry in time.

The tropics come.
Enigma follows.

Within a white room
rain in Chopin's jungle.

Orchid pinks unlimber.

In glazed porcelain bowls
floating gardenias.

Georges Sand emerges.

The charm of lace in windows.
A sundial.

High afternoon in Florence.

Romain Brooks and Natalie Barney.
The finesse of an Elinor Wylie poem.

Life is openwork
because art disarms the mundane.

There is nothing a dancer ever lacks,
but space, friends,

and confidence.

Pavan 46
  (for P.J.)

First rhyme in black
then to fashion.

Style to evoke
how the attack springs.

A knowingness that dream
is a folded map,

an oddly sequenced
disjunction.

World atrophies
without speed.

Emotion leaves
no choice.

Survive, communicate, scheme,
wait for language

to go away.

Only you vanish.

Displaced by
what cannot be,

a certainty
which like the visual

or a stasis,
satisfies
the bodiless itch

for an idiom.

Pavan 47
(for Linda)

Gaslight-blue morning-glory
winding north,

moth
spiraling in

the hayloft.

Wasp amongst yarrow.

Delight
inscribing earth-shine,

belfry
and spire.

Higher,
a bat French seaming

lacquer black.

Stairward up,
kimono wrapped,

wisp
of incense smoke.

Whisper wrapped
around oracle,

erotic,

poem congealing
under streetlights.

The street life
of a soprano.

Pavan 48
   (for Tom)

The man who believes
in cocaine and confusion

and the man who believes in art
appear in strange juxtaposition.

Paris isn't an exit
of the Hollywood Freeway

though they scripted Villon's life.

Even Gertrude Stein
would have loved to come

if she'd been sent
a proper invitation.

It's shadow and form
amongst the afterborn,

a tango that fills
archetype's last apparency,

a back street
which would have baffled

Plato.

Pavan 49
  (for W.)

As image
she belongs

to another's
imagination.

Encircled by
sophistication and silk

her scent
waters the parched
hunger of my eyes.

Grief is already taking apart
simple things.

A perfumed slip
outlined on the floor.

She whispers,
dance complies,

and I age
like a photograph
that desire develops in the dark,

a language that lust speaks
while I,

without language,
hustle her shadow.

Pavan 50
   (for Laury)

I steal a day
from stone.

Oh,
how sky is

a shine
in the roots

of language.

Strands of poems
whistle in

the desert.

Dry as lizards
they dance out

from under
the walls.

Pavan 51
  (for Carol)

Milan to L.A.
city-

scape.

(A world mapped
by figurative

art.)

Your choice
of

transfer.

The mental blocks,
imaginary neighborhoods,

the metalinguistics
of streets.

(Cuisine underlies
reality.)

Take ramps,
fashion shows,

streetlights,

window displays.

(Secret aesthetics
passed by the photo-

graphiques of
haute couture.)

A dazzling sky
between Italy

and California.

Pavan 52
 (for Llon)

Oh Nijinsky you danced
and the future came.
Madness left you where it did.
Duchamp hid.
H.D. and Ezra Pound entranced,
while in Hollywood
myth ranged higher,
to and fro,
ipso quo,
more sophisticated
and philosophically lighter
in the ever burgeoning metaphor
whose lint
is desire.

Pavan 53
  (for Robin)

Because heart is
four-chambered.

Blood in,
blood out;

blood in,
blood out;

seasons the same to light.

Because a dark slough
where terns roost

is now deserted.

Because a constructed moon
low in sky

hisses an emptiness.

Because your death
is nearsight.

Backlit eyes

trigger this world's ache,
a marrow to yearning.

Because your absence is
four irregular pieces,

scattered crags
under the bleak
final night of galaxies.

Because skull-white gulls
huddle on asphalt

drink day's final warmth.

Because without you
sun is a shrunken star.

CYCLE THREE

Pavan 54
   (for Jeanette)

I've been dismantling
day all night,

night all day,

and dreaming
tangled with my hands

as dreaming may
when it loses voice.

Now the outline
of my fingers
shapes the silence
into

"I miss you."

How can I stay simple
when I waver between
true emotion and cliche

as a poem wavers
between literal meaning

and music?

Day etches its weight
on light,

emotion dismantles
words.

Night responds to night
and is darkness.

Night responds to day
and is dream.

Dream responds to night
as Durer did

when his rendering portrayed
how hands mean,

in the deepest way,

merely by being
hands.

   Pavan 55
     (for Laurel)

Earlier
does not

exist.

The Celtic
teapot,

a knot of
sugar-white calla lilies.

Oh listen,

to the birds!

Pavan 56
   (for Maureen)

Moorish grey moon
improvises,

delights.

Wistful motion
among stone and bunchberry.

A channel
through which sound
augurs,

bevels a tune
into universe.

Presence,
quinine to body.

Orchid spike
issuing color

up from.

Brass on cold mornings.

How air
pitches a day,

slides through scale,
by conversation,

settles
like gravity

in sunlight.

Terra cotta roofs
pitched,

awash in wind.

Basques moving
in mountains.

Geography is percussive,
castanets,

basil leaves cackling in stews.

Language evolves from this,
begins with ankle.

Poem draws sun
to the cold of words,

gathers fire
from shards of object and space,

celebrates the wrinkle,
the bare back,

the wigwag.

Pavan 57
  (for Celeste)

Unbinding
a heavy thought

which peels
and pares,

unfinding dissonance
whose no-control

leaves us rushed in time.

By dancing
we see how backlog and complexity

fixed viewpoint
to our eyes.

A simple turn,
kick,

lift,

gives warmth
a greater life.

It's more than tactile
guiding us through cold and solid,

keeping us from sticking,
growing instantly old.

In turn and spin,
rise and dip,

we grow space,
break the trance,

praise the footplay
and indeterminancy

of the world.

Pavan 58
  (for T.)

Lunar years since
actually.

Mind is
vacuum packed
to time and body.

Always the threat of purpose,

collapse of leg
in gravity.

Like an unformed diamond
the past is a place never born,

the past is a scarcity.

Yet how little
we ever forget of pleasure,

as if pleasure
wasn't a trap in space.

Motion deems a limitless exchange.

Sensation makes space persist,
praises location.

Emotion untangles need.

Dance comes,
after significance and effort,

effortlessly,

makes us perceptic-like,
splendidly free

by sensation.

Pavan 59
   (for Anick)

Sharp shredded cheese
on egg.

Cut green pepper,
sliced red onion.

Sweet butter
on Irish soda bread.

Fresh-pressed cider
with cinnamon.

Yellow-green pears
dipped in dark,

almost bitter,
chocolate.

This body's caulking.

In fresh peaches,
raspberries and champagne,

the world's campaigns
are ours.

In blackberry
and olive,

wild rice and muskmelon,

we find what birth
sets us up for stalking.

Pavan 60
  (for J.)

She quickens sultriness,

colors sound in
strict white,

inhales where things
bend to ear.

She untangles space,
sheds location.

Tapping shadow and eddy
she seeds veins.

She frees the dark side of balance
from weight,

relieves the gravity
of being time born

so lengthwise and visible.

Pavan 61
  (for Maguite)

Complication strings
because being

is an uneven beat.

Rhythm entangles with uncertainty
and night goes stale.

How difficult
to communicate through

what sensation
does to space.

Verbal life
thickens

the everyday.

It's a miracle
that we move at all,

marvelous to
shake off mystery,

take off our socks,

reset scale to space,

move barefoot
through the shivering.

Pavan 62
  (for J.)

Braided plaits,
twisted and sexual

in highlight of sun.

How your back
curves down.

Who you are
isn't what you wear,

but what you wear
can be a sound.

In freckles
and dungarees,

in crease of ear,
shape of eye,

is the obstinacy
of the intricate

to be found.

Pavan 63
  (for Laury)

Coarse shore fog,
spicy Thai food.

Taste revivifies passion.

Bitterness and depth,
pale salt of desire,

tart of greeting,

and sometimes
harsh burning sweetness
of farewell,

apply a weight
to nostalgia.

Dance reveals
coverings,

recreates how
being becomes trapped

in air.

Yearning is
why we eat,

Will oxidizes
pleasure.

Love a body light,

often too weak
to heat

the stiffened
darkness.

When the shape
of universe

lies like
an unknowingly learned response
in memory,

and love
is but another

reflex of the body,

there is failure.

Dance begins
by breaking the inertia

of physical origination,

takes apart
the cliche

of control,

dissolves
false imagination.

It's only when we
create space

that space
begins to tell,

like a cuisine,

the spice
and pleasure

of our rapture.

Pavan 64
  (for Lynn)

Brain is a diffident
and stale

place.

Where sun
touches shapes

healing can't fail.

(Views mend.)

It's not body
that suffers

first break.

Illness
is a protest

culled
from the reactive data

of mistake.

It's effort
that's failed,

being's command
to flourish and survive

misapplied by some
scrambled notion.

Form confuses it
with space,

re-enacts some
unresolved mystery.

Disease is metaphor
run wild.

It cataracts,
encysts,

traps.

It's language
conceptualized

by rumor,

a grammar
that death stops

a greater threat
than a body,

that death erases
the collapse

of space.

But neither you
or the universe

vanish with death.

It's too rough,
you're too interiorized

for that.

Death is a viewpoint
that considers life

the trap.

But look how you fit.

To make this universe
go away

you first
must truly believe

in it.

Pavan 65
   (for P.J.)

In thought
the defects of words

show us other words.

Language is an itch.

Emotion may catch
at the dry,

but the eye remains wet.

The eye by-passes forget.

Like Rilke
the eye goes out

dancing.

Pavan 66
 (for (Salvador)

Music
shines with sweat.

Lizard skin boots,
a scent of saddle soap.

Bob Wills
and the Texas Playboys.

A sheepskin vest
and the sullen flash

of burnished silver.

The shiver of
cold beer and

a steel guitar.

Dance which breaks
like a curve

from the erotic.

It's all in the approach.

How on broad plains

where sunlight creaks
at fences or gates,

the range a coyote
inscribes,

all in how matter
greets the heels.

Dance floors and
a love for tits,

for copping feels.

A swing violin
dissects romance.

Your new partner
sneaks out

into the true Western night,

tries to shake down
the moon.

You're last seen
the other side of sober

trying to scale desire
without scuffing

your new boots,

pressing
to get there in time

to beat her back

into the myth
of her jeans.

Pavan 67
  (for D.)

All
that stood for all

stood still.

Wind raced past.
The end glistened.

Unlike a rabbit,
but ever so softly

your voice
brushed mine.

Words were sound no more,
but a finer affinity.

What floated was borne away.

A white sun
sank behind the curved

grey sea.

All
that was still

stood for all.

Wind raced past,
glistened.

No scarcity.
More room than in space.

What was seen
stayed.

What needed time
vanished.

What was yearned for
all along

remained still
as the fog

that sheathes
the spasm

of the final dream.

Pavan 68
 (for F.)

Abrupt physical love.

Breath presses
against

thigh.

Emotion craves
quickening.

Mind rises
to find

a nostalgia.

Intention
explains itself away,

just a self-sadness
or waste.

(In thought
I know

what I need,

but body is
a strange seed.)

It means what it seems to.

I can have you or not.

Have you and not.

Though it seems to be not.

And not is a strangely
vivid dream

culled from the falling off
of the physical.

Not is a lovely thing.
Not can be as wonderful as have.

Not can wish you well.

Not can tell you
what you might forget.

Not can say goodbye.

Not can tell you everything.

Pavan 69
  (for A.)

It's better now
then when.

Shape isn't supposition.

Take it
and it inclines

like loss.

Take it
like snow

shaping space.

Of cares and dreams
there are no end,

but your toes still curl
around the edge.

Your extremities
a fringe

to anatomy's
strange joys.

Physical love is time off.

Physical love is attenuation.

Sex the glue of connotation.

It's the prima facie
shock of force.

Orpheus made the wild beasts dance,
but Eurydice disappeared down,

Eurydice took the vacation.

It's better now
then when in time.

Was you mine last night
Amy?

Was you mine?

Pavan 70
  (for Loren)

Erotic never was
a proper history.

You're not trying
to whittle down

essence anymore,

but to find
your point,

be fresh,
newer than a mystery.

In world
movement confuses

the relative
with the absolute,

loses reference,
mockingly shifts.

It substitutes,
craves, eats,

wastes and binds,

but sometime the glorious.

Oh, the glorious!

How sound shapes morning.
The sun.

It is just so.

Just is.

Space is
a forced vacation

from the obvious,

that sex
like dance

defines,

when it ceases
to merely be

the metaphor,

when it sets
and is not set up

by time.

Pavan 71
  (for C.)

Beauty wrinkles
around your eyes,

the erotic
weight/mass of you

waits unfinished
for reply.

A dull sigh of light,
fine for objects,

but too sullen and subdued
for the body.

Nothing between us
thus complexity fills the air.

You are a difficult
reach,

an erotic gesture
inciting me up from the flat

to the steep and glorious.

Pavan 72
   (for Jeannette & Tom)

Bronze bells
in dew hue of morning.

Cold wellwater;
tongueplay amongst tastes.

Sweet astringency,
vital bitter,

succulent salt,
thrust of sour.

In the tuning of North/South
penis/papillae,

in crawl space between
female/male,

a marriage,
a dragonfly's glimmering,

a tenderness like
Taos in the Spring.

Pavan 73
  (for Larry)

Release,
not as refugee
from profusion,

but as sashay.

To chat,

strip significance
from mass,

then toy
with the resulting world.

Words rise
from swagger,

unwrap optic nerve.

Orange sneakers
by cacti,

large hibiscus.

The occultness
of fireflies

by a seesaw.

Pavan 74
  (for M.)

Rain on roof.

Genji.

Mustard and lavender Berkeley days
stretching

near to emotion.

How she at sixteen

"pulled your packet."

You from so long ago,

Telegraph Ave.,
Sausalito.

A friend's lover.
No longer a friend's lover.

No longer a friend's
lover.

Lover.

"I fell in love with potential,
but it's never together. If only
she had it all,
that same vivacity, but with focus."

Current mind breath of alcohol
and the dull.

A shine that can be reapplied.

Dream the world.

Dream magic
again.

Genji.

Mustard and Lavender.

Rain on round roof.

Hokusai's waves.

Awaken.

Breath with your eyes.

Be woman that the girl
yearned to earn.

Emotion reoccurs in time.

Will reaches.

Genji.

Basho.

Once more
the boundaries of dance.

Find your metaphor
and pride will move you

over the edge

(mustard and lavender)

into dance again.

Pavan 75
  (for Gary)

Sidereal sound
of live plucked string

resonates.

Down climbing stone stairs
to root cellar

for barrel apple.

Emotion is sight.

Slow boiling of rice
in stream water.

Wet reeds drying
to coarse paper.

Wood bowl of Zen.

Burgundy countryside
where troubadours roamed

to the taut skin sound
of drum.

Waysides of day.

What shows is dance,
is ting of tambourine
to eye,

weight of foot lifted
to scrape moss off the rock
of gravity.

Pavan 76
  (for J.)

Excited silence.
Cold spice of night
on tongue.

Solitude earthly like a dune,

not time's salted edge
or the bitterness of tea,

but a strange sweet melon.

You mingle with wild peach,
shore pine,

a flower-laden vine
living between things,

a taste I crave,

a shallow-water star
off the tilted axis

of a low
radish-white half-moon.

Pavan 77
  (for D.L.)

Dancer's tryst
shifts to conjuring.

Language willow-like.

Sunburnt nostril,
wind chilled eye.

Senses sing
how body's weight

alters objects.

Ears are listening pools.

Between cold and bright
a grammar links shape

to earthly life.

Voice an arc in air.

You move like a dancer
untying shadow

and the knot of sorrow
from words.

Pavan 78
  (for Nancy B.)

Cloud above
the rigid and lax,

above where the world
loses precision

and days won't do
what they are asked.

More fire than air.

Danger in too little future,
too much past.

We meet the way spiders
and eagles embrace the ordinary.

Pavan 79
  (for C.)

Restless,
cincture-eyed,

pliant where life light
strikes algae-darkened sea.

Woman in physique of sensation.

In air
your name
mouthed by a C.

forms like hail
in a quick chilled sky.

In the slippage of things,
in the envelope of their names

your presence grows,
a slow lichen

on my passion.

I yearn to draw
the gourd of your ear

to my throat

so you can feel
how numbness
senses sun,

why winter
goes away.

Pavan 80
  (for Loren)

In incision
between

shadow
and outrage

occlusion brings
emptiness to things.

Tangled echo
diminuendo,

web of collapse
or scarcity

where isolation
blanches sound.

In this confusion,
where one turns

as if caught
by rumor,

I find you taking apart
simple things.

Your style
the R & B of creation.

Serious dance
may begin

with the unquenchable thirst
for perfect balance
and direction.

But somewhere
in

intimate magic
of preparation

abundance gathers.

In that bountiful
rehearsal and quickening

comes the power of knowing

that true grace
comes alone

from tinkering.

Pavan 81
 (for L.R.H.)

A partner comes from silence,
guides dance from black to air.

Listening celebrates timbre,

like a fog encircling a tree
its interest loosens the weight of
centuries.

The arc is
to have, hear, and seek,

to will.

Music releases ridges that bind
this mind/body more.

Being and motion stem from a place
more infinite and simple than time.

Joy is an outward flow,
blows like heat/light
from sun.

In the bow and step of no-reach days
dance isn't the only way,

but it comes close.

Dance rebalances the as is,
loosens a grace than can

unknot the universe.